MARRIAGE CHALLENGES
for Him

*One Year of Weekly Suggestions to Love Your
Wife More Effectively and Transform Your Marriage*

MANDY SHROCK

Marriage In Abundance's Marriage Challenges for Him
© 2022 Mandy Shrock.

Library of Congress Control Number: 2022918918
ISBN: 978-1-958477-05-2 (Paperback)
ISBN: 978-1-958477-06-9 (Digital Online)

Cover and Interior Design by KUHN Design Group | kuhndesigngroup.com

First printing edition 2022.

Published by In Abundance, LLC

info@marriageinabundance.com

CONTENTS

FOREWORD

This book of suggested marriage challenges is just "one part of a whole" for Marriage In Abundance's approach to a better marriage. Our goal at Marriage In Abundance is to help couples discover just how deep and meaningful their marriage relationship can be. For best results, this book, along with *Marriage Challenges for Her,* is to be used in conjunction with *Marriage In Abundance's Date Plans for Married Couples* and *Devotions for Married Couples.* To find access to the full program, visit www.marriageinabundance.com.

Here's an overview of what you'll find through Marriage In Abundance:

- **Date Plans for Married Couples**—weekly date plans for fostering creative, engaging, quality time together.

- **Couples' Devotions**—weekly studies to deepen your spiritual connection with God and each other.

- **Marriage Challenges**—weekly suggestions for showing love to one another more effectively, plus monthly suggestions for eliminating unhealthy styles of conflict resolution. As our schedules become overloaded, marital connection takes a backseat. The marriage challenges bring intentionality to meeting one another's needs and desires and spicing up the romance.

INTRODUCTION

WHAT ARE MARRIAGE CHALLENGES?

Sometimes, in trying to meet all of life's demands, connection with our spouse takes a backseat. We fall into a routine that feels more like roommates than lovers. Unless we're intentional about keeping the connection and romance alive, the spark will dwindle. Completing the weekly marriage challenges is a way to be intentional about expressing your love for your wife amid the hustle and bustle and keeping the romance alive.

We all have different needs, desires, and ways we feel loved. Maybe hugs don't mean much to you, but her encouragement does. Maybe a gift feels meaningless compared to her showing interest in you sexually. Typically, when we express love to one another, we do so in a way we understand it, not the way someone else understands it. In trying to make our wives feel loved, we sometimes "miss the mark." Since marriage challenges touch on every avenue of showing love, if you follow our suggestions, you're sure to express love in a way your wife understands. You may even discover a new way she feels love that neither of you knew before!

In addition to the weekly challenges, which are fun ways to show affection, the once-a-month habit reformation challenges will transform your approach to conflict resolution. If you only add fun to the marriage, but don't eliminate the unhealthy habits—such as yelling, interrupting, manipulating, and name-calling—you won't experience as much growth in the marriage. As old habits die hard, you will have one month to focus on better conflict resolution before moving on to another challenge.

MARRIAGE CHALLENGE INSTRUCTIONS

Separate or Together: Most of the challenges are to be done for each other separately. For example, one week you might be challenged to give her a massage with no strings attached, while your wife is challenged to encourage you in an area you are having success. However, sometimes the challenges are to be done together. For example, be intentional about kissing every day that week. In this case, the challenge will say "together," and you can discuss and complete that challenge together. If it doesn't say "together," don't discuss your challenge, just do it.

No Peeping: It is important to keep your challenges in a place your spouse won't be peeping. We don't recommend spouses hide *anything* from each other *ever*—except for the marriage challenges. If your wife sees your challenge and you have not done it, this sets her up for disappointment and will do more harm than good. If you happen to see her challenge lying around, no snooping! Keep your mind focused on your own challenge.

Romance During Everyday Routine: The challenges can be done at any point that is convenient for you that week. However, if you are also participating in the date plans, the challenges are not meant to be done at the same time as the date. The purpose of the marriage challenges is to add intention and romance into your everyday routines, not just on your date together.

A Way to Remember: Part of the problem in keeping the romance alive in a marriage is that you aren't thinking about romance in your everyday lives. It happens to everyone. When you were dating, you were infatuated—smitten—and spent more time thinking about ways you could express love to her. But after you sealed the deal and fell into busyness, you no longer put as much thought into romance. Remembering to pick up this book each week may prove to be just as difficult. So, we suggest setting a couple alarms on your phone—one alarm to remind yourself to pick up your book and look at your challenge for the week, and a second alarm for a time you can complete your challenge that week.

Explicit Content: Considering the marriage challenge's intent is to reignite the romance, some of the challenges, or "assignments," are sexual in nature. Therefore, it is not recommended to keep your marriage challenge books in a place easily accessible to your children.

If any of the sexual marriage challenges cause friction, or trigger a negative emotional response, skip that challenge, and prayerfully consider whether there's a deeper issue that needs addressed in counseling.

Stretch and Grow: You may not feel like doing some challenges—not because it triggers a negative emotion, but because it's just not "your thing." For example, maybe you're not into dancing but your challenge is to squeeze in a slow dance after dinner on your living room floor. If you don't do your challenge simply because that's not "your thing," you are limiting growth and denying your spouse full enjoyment of you. Comfort zones are confining. You won't grow if you're not willing to stretch.

Fifth Week: There are four challenges each month. Since there is a fifth week every three months, to stay in the habit, we suggest going back and doing one you missed or doing your favorite again.

Stay Positive: When your spouse does, or says, something nice, you may think, *I bet that was her challenge this week. She only did that because she was told to do it.* Another way to look at it is, *I'm so glad my wife wants to show me love and is giving this a try!*

Make It a Lifestyle: Although the intent is for you to focus on completing one challenge per week, our hope is that, as you begin putting them into practice, these expressions of love become a part of your marriage lifestyle.

JANUARY

(Together) What have you been arguing about lately? Take a break from discussing that topic for a week. When it comes to mind, simply pray over it. Discuss it next week, only after having covered it in prayer.

(Together) In the midst of a stressful moment, hug each other and focus on your breaths. Don't end the hug until your breaths are in sync.

Out of the blue, tell her you love her and appreciate all she does for you, your family, and your home. Provide examples of what, specifically, you appreciate.

Ask her what area of her body she wants massaged, then deliver.

Write a love note on the shower door or bathroom mirror using soap or rubbing alcohol. (It will appear when steamy.)

FEBRUARY

Practice forgiving your wife quickly. Don't wait for an apology. Make peace priority in the relationship over being "right."

What topic interests her? Email her or text her a link about that topic and say, "This reminded me of you."

For Valentine's Day, instead of buying her a card, write your own. (If you get writer's block, search online for inspiration.)

Spice things up for her by applying a stimulating cream down there to enhance blood flow in that area. These can be found in grocery or drug stores. If natural ingredients are preferred, O Gel by Sliquid Organics can be found online.

Kiss her cheek while she's doing dishes. Then tell her to go sit down while you finish them.

MARCH

Don't bash your wife to your friends and family. If you need relationship advice, talk only with a trusted mentor while protecting and honoring her reputation among your family and friends.

(Together) Look into each other's eyes without saying anything for five minutes. What's the point? A scientific study suggested just two minutes of eye gazing increased mutual attraction and passion significantly. Try it to deepen your marital bond. Extra credit: Eye gaze for ten to twenty minutes!

A woman loves when her hard work is noticed. Take a moment to notice and show admiration for even the small achievements in her day. For example, the closet she cleaned out or the way she handled a conflict at work or with family. Compliment her accomplishments.

Give her a long, slow kiss. Whisper a sweet nothing in her ear. Then go in for another kiss.

(Examples of sweet nothings: *I love you. You make me happy. You look pretty. You're the only one for me. You're the best.*)

At a moment she's not bustling around, turn on music to a slow song that is special to you as a couple and ask her for a dance.

APRIL

When your wife is doing something that upsets you, try "I Statements" instead of "You Statements." "I Statements" put the focus on your feelings instead of placing blame on her. This lowers her defenses and improves communication. For example, instead of, "You keep interrupting me!" replace it with, "I feel like my thoughts aren't important when I don't get to finish expressing what's in my head." Instead of, "You're always nitpicking everything I do," try, "I feel degraded when I'm not trusted to make even the most minor decisions for myself."

(Together) Try a new breathing technique while making love. During the act, focus on your breaths. As you breathe in, arch your back while imagining your pelvic floor moving away from you. As you breathe out, think about it returning to you. This exercise heightens your awareness to the area and increases sensation.

Bring home flowers for no
reason other than you love her.

Post something about your wife
on social media to affirm and
encourage her. If you don't
use social media, write it in
a place visible to others.

While she's cooking,
ask her how you can help.

MAY

Admit an area you've been wrong. This may make us *feel* small, but in truth, it is admirable, displays maturity, and is one giant step forward for a relationship.

Fill in the blanks with a fond memory and text this statement to her, "Remember when we (or you) _____. When I think of it, I feel _____."

Lead a prayer at dinnertime.
Include in the prayer how much
you love your wife and family.

At the end of the day, when she won't be going outside the house again, brush her hair. Extra credit: Watch an online tutorial for braiding hair and give it a try.

You know that habit of yours that bothers your wife? Take a major step toward breaking that habit. Ideas: quit cold turkey, get an accountability partner, attend a support group, or get addiction counseling if it's an addiction.

JUNE

When our happiness requires something from someone else, that is unhealthy. Remove that expectation from your wife. If needed, seek outside help for depression or other issues.

(Together) Develop a new routine to spend ten to fifteen minutes each day communicating about your day. Ideas: Go for a walk after dinner or sit on the patio after the kids go to bed.

If you have kids, teach them to express love and appreciation to your wife. If you don't have kids, write your wife a short poem about your love for her.

The next time you're out in public,
wink at her from across the room.

Before you leave for work (or
on your day off) make a salad
for her lunch with her favorite
toppings and dressing. (This will
require advanced prep to ensure
you have all the ingredients.)

JULY

Don't name-call or use
words that attack your wife's
character. Remember the goal
is to resolve conflict and act as
a team, not to cause your wife
to feel defeated as a person.

(Together) Add a little romance into each day with kiss variety!

Sunday: While engaged in a sensuous kiss, suck your spouse's bottom lip.

Monday: Nibble your spouse's earlobe.

Tuesday: Kiss while one of you is upside down. (Since we're not superheroes, one of you can lie on the couch or bed.)

Wednesday: She puts on lipstick and leaves her mark.

Thursday: Give your spouse's neck some sensational attention.

Friday: Kiss for at least ten minutes while your lips and tongue explore and rediscover each other's mouth.

Saturday: Kiss while thinking tender, loving thoughts about your spouse. The difference can be surprising!

Place sticky notes all over the house
with encouraging words for her.

What quality are women typically drawn to in a man? What quality do male characters in romance novels possess? The answer is leadership. Up your game in the leadership department. Ideas: facilitate a small group, coach a kids' sports team, take charge of a family stressor, have a needed conversation with the kids, teach the kids a new skill, take on a leadership role at work.

The next time you're sitting next to
each other, reach for her hand—
hold it, gently stroke or massage it.

AUGUST

Don't interrupt. Allow your wife to finish her thoughts before speaking.

Many women love vocal affection during lovemaking. While making love, verbally express your desire for her.

For example: *You're so beautiful. I'm hungry for your love. You take my breath away. I've been thinking about your touches all day. I adore your body.*

Profess your love for her
outside using sidewalk chalk.

Surprise her with her favorite treat.

Complete her honey-do list. Schedule it in your calendar and tell her when she can expect it to get done. If something more important comes up that day, reschedule it. Make it your priority.

SEPTEMBER

Stay on the same team in parenting. If one of you makes a rule, the other supports it. If you disagree with your spouse's parenting decision, talk about it in private—not in front of the kids—and then present your agreed-upon decision to the kids, together as a husband-wife team. Not only is it important for kids to have consistency, but for a family to be healthy, the marriage relationship needs to be stronger than the parent-child relationship.

(Together) Worship together and lift your marriage up to God while worshipping. This can be through either a personal experience in your home or during the church worship service.

Buy her something to support her hobby. Ideas: gadgets, classes, a book about her hobby, or that thing she's been wanting to get for it.

Hug her for at least ten
seconds every day this week.

Text her, "I love your [insert
your favorite personality trait]."

OCTOBER

During a disagreement, try this new communication technique: Listen carefully to your wife, then confirm back to her, in your own words, what you heard her saying. This is not to say you agree but are giving an earnest attempt to see things from her perspective. If you misunderstood her, it helps her to know she needs to change her wording. When you repeat it back, make sure not to interject your own feelings but convey you understand how she is feeling. For example, "What I hear you saying is that [paraphrase what you heard] and it makes you feel [describe how she feels]."

(Together) Change up the place you usually make love. Ideas: the office, the car, a different room of the house.

Pray and thank God for all the people who invested in your wife and helped her become the woman she is today. If her mom is living, send her mom flowers with a note saying, "Thank you for your lovely daughter." (Don't tell your wife you did this. Let her mom tell her.)

Place a love letter on her pillow.

Pay attention to her feelings. When she seems tired, drained, and stressed, ask what is exhausting her and take one burden off her plate.

NOVEMBER

(Usually, "Habit Reformations" are done together. This month, they are separate challenges.) Gently, but firmly, keep family members from disrespecting her.

(Together) In most marriages, passionate kissing and long make-out sessions end shortly after marriage. Bring it back! Go into a locked room or closet and have a prolonged make-out session with no sexpectations.

(Extra credit: The next time you are out in public together, sneak into a corner or a bathroom for a quick "kiss & pet" session.)

Pay attention to comments she makes about things she likes, wants, or needs so you can buy her a Christmas gift that says *I pay attention to you.*

Make a "jar of endearments." On small pieces of paper, write encouragement for her. Tell her to pull out a few the next time she has a bad day. Ideas: traits you like in her, special memories that bring her joy, her favorite Scriptures, reminders of her past successes, encouragement regarding her giftings and skills, your gratitude for her.

The next time you are walking together in public, place your hand on her hip or low back.

DECEMBER

Do not belittle your wife. Making her feel small will only wedge you apart. If an issue needs addressed, discuss it only after you've had a chance to calm down and without degrading her character.

Pray for a specific
success for your wife.

What does your wife do well? Point it out to her. (She probably doesn't know.) Include examples.

Make a hot bath for her with candles and soft music. Extra credit: Stick her towel in the dryer for ten minutes and bring it to her fresh and warm.

Surprise her by cleaning the
house while she's gone.

CONCLUSION

We hope you were able to find new ways to express love to each other and were brought closer together on this journey of marriage challenges. If you haven't already, consider participating in the full package of Marriage In Abundance, including date plans and couples' devotions. Find out how by visiting www.marriageinabundance.com. Stay tuned as there will be a second book with another year of fun and bonding activities coming soon!

ABOUT THE AUTHOR

Mandy Shrock is the founder of Marriage In Abundance, a ministry aimed at deepening the bonds of married couples. In addition to writing materials for marriage improvement, she also wrote, *Life In Abundance,* devotions for anyone, no matter their stage in life. She is passionate about life, the Word of God, marriage, sci-fi and fantasy books, exercise, the outdoors, natural foods, and dogs. Powered by coffee, she lives with her husband, four children, and two dogs in northern Indiana.

Printed in Great Britain
by Amazon